I0191575

THE
WIND IS
WAITING

A Christian Flight Manual

Isaiah 40:31

by Gary H. Patterson

Copyright Information

The Wind is Waiting - A Christian Flight Manual

© 2016 by Gary H. Patterson

Unless otherwise indicated, all scripture quotations are
from The Holy Bible, New King James® (NKJ®)
Unless otherwise indicated, all definitions were taken
from the Strong's Concordance of the Online Bible
Edition
Publishing by Good News Fellowship Ministries
Used by permission. All rights reserved.

Copyright © 2016 by
Good News Fellowship Ministries
220 Sleepy Creek Rd.
Macon, GA 31210

ISBN: 978-1-888081-36-7
1-888081-36-8

No part of this book may be reproduced or transmitted
in any form or by any means, electronic or mechanical,
including photocopying, recording, or by an information storage and retrieval system, without permission in
writing from the author.

Cover designed by Grace Patterson
Formatting by Lisa Walters Buck

Acknowledgments

A special thank-you to my dear wife, Teresa, who is always supportive and to my precious daughter, Grace, who did an excellent job assisting the editing of this book. I am also very grateful to our beloved prayer group whose fellowship is more precious than gold.

Contents

Preface

To help answer some questions the reader may incur while reading this book, I recommend these companion articles from our website: http://www.greatgrace4u.com: "The Most Neglected Promise," "The Baptism with the Holy Spirit," "The Sovereignty of God and Christian Responsibility," "Did Jesus Die for Our Healing?," "The Excellence of the New Covenant," and "The Lord Chastens Whom He Loves." These articles are included in the *Anchored in the Truth Series* in the "Gary's Study" section of the website.

Writing this book was an incredible journey. It was inspired by one brief encounter with nature. Nothing can compare to the inspiration of the Holy Spirit and in fact, within just a few minutes of writing this, the Lord conveyed to me,

"I love working with you too and with anyone who will open the door of communication unto Me" (Revelation 3:20).

Do you hear the heart of the Lord? Can you imagine what this indicates to you and me? It means we are wealthier than we realize.

This is not a book that will teach you how to defeat the devil and his hordes, at least not directly. Jesus has already defeated them and made a public spectacle of them (Colossians 2:13-15).

> *"Yet in all these things we are more than conquerors through Him who loved us" (Romans 8:37).*

We have already gained surpassing victory because the Father in Heaven placed His love upon us through His beloved Son. By God's grace, through faith, we have been made joint-heirs with Christ Jesus the Lord, and He is not ashamed to call us His brothers and sisters (Romans 8:17; Hebrews 2:11). This book focuses on living in this world as joint-heirs with Christ and as more than conquerors through His love for us. Being made more than conquerors was penned in context alongside the hardships that we all have faced and those we will face in this life because the devil is still the god of this world (2 Corinthians 4:3-4). His insidious rule will end when Jesus returns in wrath against him to claim what is His (Romans 8:34-36). Hardships are those things in life that bring us face-to-face with the limitations of our humanity and its frailty. While the devil will attempt to use those hardships against us, we can instead find God whose strength is perfected in our weakness. His righteousness, peace, joy, and healing displaces our disillusionment, sadness, confusion, and sickness.

Who is better equipped to ascend a great mountain: a well-equipped mountain climber, or a bird of prey such as a hawk or eagle?

The bird of prey more than conquers the mountain.

Which would you rather be?

Introduction

From the perspective of our Creator, human imagination is a powerful force which can be utilized for either good or evil purposes. In His estimation, there is nothing a united and ungodly people could imagine that would be impossible to them. This is why He created language barriers among the people at Babel. Previously, everyone spoke one language. However, they became too independently intelligent for their own good and turned against their Creator; their minds were clouded with pride at the thought of "reaching the heavens" with a mighty man-made tower (Genesis 11).

Knowing the importance of human imagination, Jesus often presented life-changing insight from the Kingdom of Heaven in the form of similes, making the Kingdom of Heaven easier to grasp. The Holy Spirit used something familiar to the listeners, appealing to their imaginations, when revealing important truths. For example, Matthew 13 states:

> *"The Kingdom of Heaven is like a grain of mustard seed..."*

"The Kingdom of Heaven is like unto leaven..."

"The Kingdom of Heaven like unto a net..."

Listen to the psalmist:

"The Heavens declare the glory of God; and the firmament shows and proclaims His handiwork. (2) Day after day pours forth speech, and night after night shows forth knowledge. (3) There is no speech nor spoken word [from the stars]; their voice is not heard. (4) Yet their voice [in evidence] goes out through all the earth, their sayings to the end of the world. Of the heavens has God made a tent for the sun, (5) which is as a bridegroom coming out of his chamber; and it rejoices as a strong man to run his course. (6) Its going forth is from the end of the heavens, and its circuit to the ends of it; and nothing [yes, no one] is hidden from the heat of it" (Psalms 19:1-6; AMPC).

Creation itself emanated from God's knowledge, wisdom, and imagination. Every day and night, even though in a corrupted state (See Romans 8:19-22), His creation "talks" to us and reveals Him. God's "fingerprints" are evident in every aspect of it. Jesus used the things of creation and those common to human life symbolically as a transport to convey His Kingdom truths in a manner that people could grasp. Alleged "deeper truths" in symbolism should never distract us from the Holy Spirit's simple yet profound and liberating truth. The revelation of the truths of God's Kingdom flows unrestricted to those who value them, who, as babes, hunger and thirst for more of Him (Matthew 5:6, 11:25). Our posture before the Lord to receive understanding of His Kingdom truths should be similar to that of elementary school children, who, when the teacher asks for a volunteer and promises to give them a treat for their participation, jump up from their seats and raise their hands saying with great excitement, "Pick me, pick me, pick me!"

Scripture tells us that much of the Old Covenant and its observances (as defined in the Old Testament) used symbolism to foreshadow the Christ to come (Colossians 2:17; Hebrews 8:5 and 10:1). It served as a tutor, preparing people for the New Covenant (Galatians 3:22-27). God commanded His people to often perform specific symbolic acts in the Old Testament in order to imprint within their hearts and minds the inescapable need for the Messiah. The symbolism chosen by God left a permanent mark within the minds of the Israelites, influencing the entirety of human life.

As was required in the Old Covenant, imagine having to shed the blood of the innocent (animals) every day because of sin. The amount of carnage demanded would have been unimaginable and unforgettable, especially for fulfilling the requirements for hundreds of thousands of people. Think about that. By reading just the first chapter in the book of Leviticus, we understand the details required by God of Israel. The symbolic acts deeply imprinted this one truth in their hearts:

> *"Without the shedding of blood, there is no remission of sin" (Hebrews 9:22).*

"Remission" conveys the idea that the sinner is released from bondage or prison because their sins have been pardoned, and consequently, the penalty is set aside as if the person never committed them. The price has been paid for them through the spilling of blood.

God is neither ambiguous nor capricious but, nonetheless, remains a mystery to all who do not humbly seek after Him. He is hidden only from those who value their own intelligence above anything else, refusing to humble their minds to the influence of the Holy Spirit. God is definable in simple terms. The fact that He can be described so simply makes that simplicity so much more profound, thereby perplexing those who are wise in their own eyes—those who attempt to understand Him through human knowledge alone (1 Corinthians 1). Light, wind, oil, fire, vines, fruit, water, treasure, animals, trees, farmers, stewards, kings, servants, and shepherds are used discreetly by God to unveil Himself and His truths to us. These images do not define nor confine Him; rather, He describes Himself, and the riches we have been freely given in Christ, through them (1 Corinthians 2:12). Just as Christ declares Himself "the Light of the world," so He commands His people to "let your light shine" unto others (John 8:12; Matthew 5:16). Light does not define nor limit God. Instead, it affirms His character, for He is light and all that is good, as He defines goodness. We, as Christ's followers, are to reflect Him (light) to those around us. Just as the Biblical metaphors of light reveal who God is to us, so do Old Testament commandments like animal sacrifice.

In the Old Covenant, the people understood what a sacrificial lamb represented. In the New Testament, we find John the Baptist heralding Jesus to Israel as the Lamb of God who would take away the sins of the world (John 1:29-36). As if to say all other previous revelations of God's love were incomplete, the Apostle John later affirms:

> *"In this the love of God was manifested toward us, that God has sent His only begotten Son into the world, that we might live through Him. (10) In this is love, not that we loved God, but that He loved us and sent His Son to be the propitiation [appeasement] for our sins" (1 John 4:9-10).*

Jesus, as the sacrificial Lamb of God, is God's prize revelation. Can you imagine how proud God the Father is of His Son and of those who honor Him as He is honored in Heaven? What treasures await those who do!

Again, from Matthew 13:

"The Kingdom of Heaven is like treasure hidden in a field, which a man found and hid; and for joy over it he goes and sells all that he has and buys that field."

We end up with what we value and love the most, along with the rewards or the consequences. Your state in life is the sum total of what you have relied on in the past. What a treasure we have in Christ, and woe be unto us if we are not good stewards of it. If you have been born again of the incorruptible seed of God's Word, the means to know Him intimately is already in you (1 Peter 1:23; 1 John 2:27). To know Him deeply is to love Him with deliberate and reckless abandon, without pretense. As you will see later, doing so is not difficult. The devil, the adversary of your soul, works overtime to make the simplicity (purity, wholeheartedness, sincerity) of devotion to Christ into something complex within your thinking and believing. What devil-inspired outlooks are you tolerating (2 Corinthians 11:1-4)?

Perhaps you are someone who thinks, "I'm not a super-Christian or spiritual giant." Do you suppose that those whom you esteem as such, think that they are? Jesus prayed this to His Father in Heaven:

"I do not pray for these alone, but also for those who will believe in Me through their word; (21) that they all may be one, as You, Father, are in Me, and I in You; that they also may be one in Us, that the world

may believe that You sent Me. (22) And the glory which You gave Me I have given them, that they may be one just as We are one: (23) I in them, and You in Me; that they may be made perfect in one, and that the world may know that You have sent Me, and have loved them as You have loved Me" (John 17:21-23).

Perhaps you have become too familiar and accustomed with the way things currently are in your life. You are neither hot nor cold in your spiritual walk and have no strong motivation for the things of God. Your Father in Heaven is working now to bathe you with love, life-changing spiritual perspective, passion, identity, and destiny. Expect the Holy Spirit to make adjustments in your heart and mind as you continue to read.

While sitting in our living room talking with my wife, I received a visitation from the Lord. The way to best describe the experience is that I felt like someone (probably an angel) was standing over me and pouring warm honey over my (spiritual) heart. The fog lifted from my mind, and my heart became very much at ease and assured. Words can hardly describe the experience, but His love was like warm honey. Your Father in Heaven will minister to you exactly what is needed and sometimes when you least expect it. He does not tempt you with good things and then never deliver on His promises. The Lord is not the source of any voice or standard of living that always demands something from you but can never be appeased. Lasting and true

satisfaction and fulfillment will never be found in anything this life has to offer. You should never settle for
anything less than being God's workmanship created
in Christ Jesus. God has already prepared everything
needed for you on your journey of reflecting His goodness (Ephesians 2:10).

**Do you realize that Jesus' desire for you and
me is that we mirror to the world the same relationship and fellowship He had with His Father?
During His ministry on earth, Jesus wanted the
world to know that the Father loves you and me
just as the Father loves Him.**

No one person has a greater right of access than
another to the Kingdom of God. We all have equal access by faith into this most excellent grace in which we
stand and rejoice in hope of [continually experiencing]
the glory of God (Romans 5:1-2). The one prerequisite
is that we come before His throne of grace with a faith
that derives its boldness solely from the shed blood of
Jesus Christ (Hebrews 4:14-16; 10:15-25). He declared,
"It is finished" just before His last breath (John 19:28-
30). Three days later, He rose from the grave. His work
of redeeming us from sin and its effects is finished. Faith
excludes boasting in anything except that finished work
of Christ (Romans 3:21-31). There are no spiritual gi-
ants or super-Christians in the Kingdom of God. They
only exist in the minds of those who compare themselves with other people. Others will intimidate you or

provoke you to jealousy, but Jesus will give you remedial understanding and inspire, transform, and solidify you for His service.

Are you ready to be a mirror of that same great love that the Father has for His only begotten Son? As you read, expect the Lord to activate the spirit of wisdom and revelation of Christ within your heart. Refuse the common temptation to try to understand the things of God's Kingdom; instead look to the Holy Spirit to give you understanding. Begin to believe right now that your mind, emotions, imaginative ability, and desires are severed from the influence of your past, the flesh, and the powers of darkness. Verbally renounce and break every chain and false yoke that is self-imposed: whatever comes from offense, sinful addictive behavior, religion, human traditions and control, witchcraft, sorcery, man-made doctrines, intellectual and religious pride and prejudice, and any wrong perceptions of God and His New Covenant provisions. Choose Christ's easy and light yoke (lordship) that gives rest to your soul. Do this by the cleansing power of Jesus' blood and in His wonderful name.

A psalm (inspired by and set to the tune of "Pure Imagination" as sung by the late actor Gene Wilder):

Come with me and you'll see

A world of truth and revelation.

What you'll see

Will defy human explanation.

We'll begin with an expectant grin

Because of Christ's wonders and grace.

And we'll end with His glory

Shining from our face.

It is time for you to find your wings and fly.

Chapter I

The Hawk

Technically, a hawk is any small to medium sized bird of prey and encompasses any species of birds belonging to the Accipitridae family, including eagles, buzzards, kites, and others. The hawk species that we recognize as named are some of the most intelligent of all birds. Their advanced vision can see the visible part of the spectrum, the ultraviolet part, as well as polarized light, and magnetic fields and is around eight times more acute than a human's. In flight, a hawk will rapidly flap its wings, then glide from its own momentum, reaching speeds of over 150 miles per hour and soaring for very long periods of time. (https://en.wikipedia.org/wiki/Hawk & https://www.beautyofbirds.com/hawks.htm)

I watched an event transpire that has often proven to be a source of great encouragement for others and myself. I heard the sound of the hawk somewhere in the vast blue sky. Some of you have heard it before. My eyes explored the distance for the majestic bird and finally found it, accompanied by two haranguing crows. During the entirety of the event, the hawk never flinched once to protect itself but only adjusted its wings to change direction. Then he found it—an updraft of air. The hawk began to spiral upward without even slightly flapping its wings. The pesky crows continued their exhausting pursuit, but the hawk went to a place where they could not follow. Its faith in its wings, its momentum, and the updraft, took it much higher than the crows could ever reach through their greatest efforts.

Obviously, the hawk had been there before— It already knew how high it could soar.

Laws exist that govern the natural flight of birds and human inventions as well. The law of lift and thrust (or aerodynamics and propulsion) is what allows a bird or an airplane to overcome the law of gravity. A hawk that is poised to take flight from ground level has to generate enough thrust in its wings to overcome the initial resistance of the law of gravity until it reaches flight sustaining momentum or the wind. The rapid thrust of its wings creates the momentum that allows it to glide gracefully through the air. It knows that stagnate air at ground level and gravity is no match for its wings. The hawk knows the wind is waiting, and that its wings were made for soaring.

The hawk evaded the crows' onslaught with little effort because of its natural instinct, perfected skills, and fluency in flight. God so perfectly equipped it that no room was left for fear or failure.

The hawk knew…

- It had wings and the purpose for them.

- It could rise above the earth by using them.

- It could not rise from the earth without working them.

By now, the lights are already coming on within your understanding. You know you are supposed to be like that hawk.

Do you think that Satan, the present god of this world would want you to know that God has **spiritually** equipped you in Christ correspondingly to that of the hawk (2 Corinthians 4)? Would he want you to become knowledgeable, fluent, secure, safe, and strongly confident in this life as a hawk is in flight, contrary to and overcoming the downward pull of this world?

What is holding you back? What is weighing you down? Could this be your time to break the chains with which this world has held you down? What is keeping you from mounting up with the wings that God has promised to those who worshipfully wait on Him (Isaiah 40:31)? No onslaught, weapon, or bondage this world—or the powers of darkness—can muster against us come even close to the **terrifying** skill-set made available to us in Christ Jesus. Yes, those skill-sets **are** terrifying to the powers of darkness.

When the children of Israel sent spies into Jericho before its walls fell, they learned that the fear of Israel had already fallen upon the whole city because of their obedience to God. A woman named Rahab, who hid the spies in Jericho for their protection, told them:

> *"I know that the LORD has given you the land, that the terror of you has fallen on us, and that all the inhabitants of the land are fainthearted because of you. (10) For we have heard how the LORD dried up the water of the Red Sea for you when you came out of Egypt, and what you did to the two kings of the Amorites who were on the other side of the Jordan, Sihon and Og, whom you utterly destroyed. (11) And as soon as we heard these things, our hearts melted; neither did there remain any more courage in anyone because of you, for the LORD your God, He is God in heaven above and on earth beneath" (Joshua 2:9-11).*

Even so, Christ's death, resurrection, and ascension are already known by the powers of darkness, causing that same paralyzing effect upon the devil and his minions. Those who walk in the full assurance of faith in Christ's victory, being filled with the Holy Spirit, will understand what this means experientially. The devil does not want you to know that he is scared—that his heart and courage have melted away. He does not want you to know that you are more than a conqueror through Christ Jesus because of the love He has set upon us. No, he wants you to believe he is like the great dragon depicted in the book of Revelation. This depiction in Scripture of the devil as a vicious fire breathing beast only serves as a symbol, revealing what those who persistently exalt instead of humble themselves before their Creator will turn into.

The Israelites carried Divine judgment against their enemies wherever they went, enforcing it as the Lord instructed. Resistance to their conquest was futile. Wherever they went, it was evident that God had already been there, preparing the way. Likewise, we have been equipped in Christ because He went before us and defeated all temptation, the works of darkness, and death itself. **That same undefeatable life of Christ is in those who believe**. We can radiate that same judgment against the spiritual powers of darkness. The ruler of this world (the devil) is judged (John 16:11). He must bow the knee to those in whose heart Christ reigns.

A hawk is a terror to any prey whether on the ground or in the air. Once its keen vision has spotted the target, no mercy will be shown. Likewise, a similar fierceness is continually available for God's people that enables them to fulfill Jesus' purpose for becoming human—to destroy the works of the devil (1 John 3:8).

> *"The wicked flee when no one pursues, but the righteous are bold as a lion" (Proverbs 28:1).*

This illustration of fierce boldness parallels what was seen in Jesus when He healed the man with a withered hand on the Sabbath (Mark 3:1-6). After questioning the Pharisees, who watched with vicious intent, as to whether it was right to do good or evil on the Sabbath, Jesus looked at them with anger because of the hardness of their hearts. At the same time, He was moved with compassion toward the man with the withered hand and healed him. Being angry and compassionate at the same time seems contradictory. How can this happen? Jesus' act proves that Godly compassion must often be fueled by Godly anger in order for that compassion to find fulfillment; otherwise, it would be frustrated because of resistance from diabolical religious forces. That fierceness as seen in Christ Jesus is also available in all who believe—who partake of His Divine nature (2 Peter 1:1-4). The lack of such a wonder results in a weak church that offers hope to the world but can seldom deliver.

Do you need to break through some walls of resistance in your life? Ask Christ for His fierceness to arise within and upon you. There has to be a Godly and angry compassion in your life in order to grow into spiritual maturity—arising to new levels in Christ Jesus. That compassion will help those who are worthy of it and rebuke those who are not. Otherwise, you will tolerate things Christ would never tolerate. Expect it to arise within you as you read this book. Without it, you will hardly get off the ground.

Even as such fierceness exists naturally within a hawk, you will find that it exists as a holy resoluteness and compassion in you, having been born again of the incorruptible seed of the Word of God.

By natural instinct, a hawk already knows how to soar effortlessly upon the wind and updrafts. Of course, it does this primarily to fiercely hunt for prey, but we do it by a fierce love instinct. Even as the open skies call out to the hawk to come up higher, we are called to rise upward in Christ who is so attractive, excellent, and full of wonder. If you claim to be of Christ, and call upon the Father in His name, what is holding you back? What is your excuse? Too much of a failure? Perhaps, you are too much in control or have learned to cope with things on your own? Have you made "treaties" with things you should be conquering, resulting in unnecessary and endless battles in your life? (Read about King Asa: 2 Chronicles 14-16.)

One day, long ago, I remember being very discouraged and told the Lord that I felt like my whole life had

been a failure. His response was, "I did not expect anything else from you." Upon receiving that simple but
profound revelation, I fell back on my bed and began
to laugh. He set me free indeed from a burden He had
already carried for me to the cross. I just needed to
see things from His perspective. My Father in Heaven
caused me to fly.

Failure is a prerequisite to experiencing God-em-
powered success. God will bring you to a place where
you are deeply convinced that even success apart from
Him is failure. Self-empowered success is delusional
because it gives superficial and short-term satisfaction
but always keeps you looking in the wrong places for
something more.

> *"He gives power to the weak, and to those who have
> no might He increases strength" (Isaiah 40:29).*

When the veil of disillusionment is lifted from your
eyes in the place of difficulty as you call upon the name
of the Lord, you can rise up in faith and receive Christ's
strength that endures all things with great joy and peace
(Romans 5:13). That joy and peace cannot be found in
other people, the world, or ourselves, because it only
originates in Christ. It only comes to those who surrender to the easy yoke of His lordship that gives rest to
every part of us (Matthew 11:25-30).

Are you tired of seeing your best efforts in life frustrated? Need to break the patterns of failure and spir-

itual stagnation of the past? What about healing for a lingering physical ailment that will not quit? Is there an offense that you are still carrying that may hinder deliverance from anything else? I remind you of what Jesus said,

> *"Blessed is he who is not offended because of Me"* *(Matthew 11:6; Luke 7:23).*

Those words were sent to John the Baptist who was awaiting a death sentence in prison because his preaching convicted the unrighteous and self-righteous of their sins. Jesus' words were not too comforting. Comfort will only come from the Lord after you have faced and embraced the sometimes hard-to-swallow truth about yourself. Although you may not be facing an inevitable death sentence like John the Baptist, just living in this world subjects you to many opportunities of offense that can become sources of disillusionment. Like John, you may then become self-absorbed and lose sight of who Christ really is. The reality of His being with and for you can become vague. To help prevent this, you must often shout, "Christ has not left me alone. HE IS alive from the dead, and His resurrection is giving life to every part of me!"

> *"Great peace [Hebrew word shalom; an overall sense of well-being] have they who love Your law; nothing shall offend them or make them stumble" (Psalms 119:165; AMPC).*

Absolutely loving the truth of Christ will prove your stability and integrity when facing offenses. When you and your gifts are overlooked by and not valued by people, God is watching to see if you will remember who you are in Christ or let such experiences define you. What defines you? Your place in the home? Your job? Your place or title in a church? What about certain people's praise or criticism? What about your being under the "authority" of certain spiritual leaders? Is that what defines you? If so, you are being set up for serious offense, bewilderment, and disillusionment. God sees what people do not. The Greatest Being in the universe (and outside of it) will always give you an audience if you approach boldly by the blood of His precious Lamb. What greater praise and honor is there if He applauds you? All you need do is say,

"Father in Heaven, I come before you only because of Jesus' precious blood. I desire to honor Him as you do because you raised Him from the grave and seated Him at your right hand."

Your Father in Heaven will never overlook you if you honor His Son as He does, denouncing rival dependencies on your best efforts, intelligence, physical charm, social status, and position in a church.

A hawk can become disoriented and severely injured in storms if it does not lock itself with its feet and toes to the limb of a large tree. It must also often oil its feathers with its bill from a gland on its body to keep its inner layer of protective feathers from becoming wet. Likewise, Jesus is your immovable and mighty oak tree of protection. His anointing (oil) keeps the elements of the world from harming you. (Remember the five wise and five foolish virgins - Matthew 25.) Cling to Christ, expecting fresh anointing from His presence. Do that now before continuing. Tell Him what you expect. Be bold about it because He wants to commune with and freshly anoint you beyond imagination.

Make Christ your sole refuge because all that this world has to offer is sinking sand.

You can arise to your place of immunity in Christ, whether storm or calm, not by great effort, but by finding, understanding, and becoming fiercely confident with the "wings," the "wind," and the "shelters" He has already provided. Ready to rise in Christ's unfailing love for you? Once you begin, you will realize that failure is not in the vocabulary of your new nature in Christ.

Chapter II

The "∂a Vinci" Longing

What was the Holy Spirit indicating when He spoke through the Prophet Isaiah that we would mount up with wings as eagles and not become weary or faint?

> *"Have you not known? Have you not heard? The everlasting God, the LORD, The Creator of the ends of the earth, neither faints nor is weary. His understanding is unsearchable. (29) He gives power to the weak, and to those who have no might He increases strength. (30) Even the youths shall faint and be weary, and the young men shall utterly fall, (31) but those who wait on the LORD shall renew their strength; they shall mount up with wings like eagles, they shall run and not be weary, they shall walk and not faint" (Isaiah 40:28-31).*

Hasn't God promised you "wings" to navigate the wonders of who He is? Here is an appropriate quote from Leonardo da Vinci:

"For once you have tasted flight, you will walk the earth with your eyes turned skywards, for there you have been and there you will long to return."

That statement symbolically spotlights a deep and often ambiguous longing that exists within every human being. Whether you believe in the existence of the Creator God or not, something inwardly nags on you, urging you to be better, to improve, to excel, to achieve, to reach your highest potential in the context of your passionate pursuits, if indeed you know what they are. That yearning compels us to believe that there is more to life than this.

No human being was born to fly on the same level as the "crows." We all are potential hawks. Nonbelievers must honor God's Son, Jesus Christ, as He is honored in Heaven. That is how you get your wings. You must be born again of the incorruptible seed of God's Word (1 Peter 1:23). Here is God's order (Acts 2:38):

- Repentance (deliberately separating oneself) from sin, self-serving, and the world, thereby embracing Christ's lordship.

- A public expression of that repentance and the full surrender of the body to Christ's lordship through water baptism.

- Holy Spirit baptism as received by Jesus in the Jordan River (John 1:26-34) and by the disciples as Christ commanded (Acts 1-2).

Then comes the development of relationships with those who already know how to use their "wings" and find the updrafts of the Holy Spirit. The "wings" are your faith actively and fiercely embracing, admiring, and honoring the finished work of Christ on the cross and His resurrection from the grave. Walking in this effectively to produce results comes from a deep conviction that your overall wellbeing depends on it. Wholeness and soundness within the mind of a person can only come by total surrender to Christ's lordship. Only in Him are you a complete and sound human being (Colossians 2:8-10).

Every initial thrust of your wings of faith corresponds to your spirit breathing in the atmosphere of who Christ is and realizing your joint inheritance with Him. The more we operate in the Spirit of wisdom and revelation of the knowledge of the Lord Jesus Christ, the higher we rise (Ephesians 1:17-21). As you work your wings, meditating in God's written word, the Holy Spirit will reveal pertinent truths about Christ and give you wisdom for the future (John 16). You will begin to truly see with hawk-like precision. While doing this, the Spirit of the Lord will direct you over time into lifelong relationships and fellowship with other "hawks" of similar purpose and destiny.

Too few understand these things. Many exhaust themselves by "rowing their boats" instead of lifting up their "sails" of faith in Christ's finished work and His last will and testament (the New Covenant). Others have become far removed from their hawk-like abilities in Christ by subjecting themselves to the wrong voices that dethrone their place in Christ with mixtures of religion and humanism.

As so accurately portrayed by actor Al Pacino in the movie, *The Devil's Advocate*, Lucifer (a.k.a. the devil, Satan, the accuser of the brethren) claims to be the ultimate humanist. "I'm a fan of man!" he insists. He further insists that, while God has forsaken man, he has been there for him from the beginning. *Viewer discretion strongly advised against the entire movie.

Lucifer probably said similar things to the angels who fell with him. I am sure he also championed the angelic cause as he supposedly does the human cause even now. Can you hear his rants?

"You can be like gods—independent, self-ruling. I will give you the knowledge to make it on your own. You don't need some aloof 'God' who has left you to fend for yourself. I will show you how to empower yourself. You are already god-like. God obviously does not want or need you. You're an outcast!"

Predictably, he always leaves out the part about John 3:16. Jesus is God's irrefutable proof that He is for humankind and is not aloof, ambiguous, or capricious.

Even the things we do not understand about God can be unveiled by seeking Him for the answers through His Spirit and written word. We can now be reconciled to God through the death of His Son. Christ's ultimate sacrifice is perfect and matchless love. That act alone silences Lucifer's deluded rants. So, WHEN you whole-heartedly embrace Christ's finished work on the cross, often meditating on it, THEN the devil's rants will become INEFFECTIVE against you, just as the serpent's venom was rendered powerless against the children of Israel when they looked at the bronze serpent on the pole (Numbers 21:7-9; John 3:14-17).

Unfortunately, too much of what is now called the Christian Church has bought into the lie that we cannot personally walk with the Father as Jesus did. A man-made religious system that honors God with its lips and outward showiness has muddied the waters of that truth and how it is accomplished. It leaves people impervious to an intimate relationship with Christ. These man-made systems become the sources of identity for those who are naively enslaved to them. In these systems, the placebo of the approval of man that ministers death displaces God's life-giving approval within the Church. More care is given to pleasing people than to holding people to the conditions for discipleship. The word of God is thereby rendered powerless in people by attributing more authority to the traditions, teachings, religiously educated intellect of people, human senti-ment, and to the fabricated hierarchal structure, than to

Christ's supreme headship over the Church. They may even laud the Scriptures as entirely inspired by God, but only as a cloak to hide their insecurities and self-made images (Mark 7:6-13). This is nothing other than religious humanism—insecure humanity clothed in the grandeur of its independent and self-ruling religious proficiency.

Oh yes, there is proficiency and excellence outside of entire dependency on God, yet its integrity rests solely upon the expertise, bias, praise, and critique of those who built the operating structures for such to happen. Their human control and empowerment is the energy that makes it work. Whatever is built by people must be maintained by them and whatever is built by God is maintained by Him (Psalms 127:1). Whatever is built by God honors only Him and His workmanship and has His favor on it. Whatever originates from man only honors man in spite of it having the appearance of honoring God (John 7:8). Those who live to appease such fabricated structures have man's favor and are man-pleasers. In this life, we are classified as either man-pleasers or God-pleasers. Which one are you? What did the Apostle Paul say in Galatians 1:10-12?

The greatest delusion in the Church is the mixture of Biblical truth with man-made teachings that anesthetize the people to the fullness of Christ. They are charmed by the teachings to believe they already have all they need. Such teachings give them a false sense of security while leaving them demonically oppressed, sick, diseased, and powerless for change on any level. God's approval rests only upon the truth from His word that has not been twisted to fit a certain religious bias common to a church denomination, Bible teacher, or to limited religious experience and practice. If we engage God according to His New Covenant, He will honor it. If we attempt to engage God contrary to that covenant, no matter how persuasive the teachings, we will reap from what we honor the most.

The "God who works in mysterious ways" is no mystery, whereas, He has been revealed in human form through His Son, Christ Jesus (John 1). While He may do things beyond your understanding, He never desires to leave us in the dark. Holy Scripture bears witness to who He is and the many things He did and still desires to do. It also reveals the fact that we can do the same works and greater because He ascended to the Father in Heaven and is now seeking to work through many Holy Spirit-filled people. His works in the earth are no longer limited to just one human body/temple but to the many who are in Christ Jesus (John 14-16).

From all of this, we can conclude that whatever originates from man, even if it has the appearance of being from God, will not truly satisfy the "da Vinci longing" within.

Before He ascended back to His Father, Jesus assured us that He would not leave us as orphans but gave the promise of the Comforter, the Holy Spirit (John 14-16). Having received the promise of the Father on the Day of Pentecost, the early Church began to soar. Their "da Vinci longing" could then be entirely satisfied and not frustrated. They were endued (clothed) with supernatural power to operate in this life as did Jesus with a hawk-like fierceness and compassion that could not be stopped. Only with that power can we soar in Christ. Have you obeyed the Lord Jesus and received the Holy Spirit as they did on Pentecost? Without that experience, you will barely get off the ground.

Fabricated religion only gives a placebo of hope for such things—always requiring something of us but never truly providing Heaven's help. Jesus was clothed with power after being baptized by John in the Jordan River, and His disciples, at least one hundred and twenty of them, received that same power on the day of Pentecost. Consequently, they began do the same and even greater works as promised (John 14:12-13).

The last will and testament left to us by Christ is lovingly and fervently enforced by Him as the risen Savior, the Great High Priest, and the fierce King of Kings. Our faith in Him is our wings (or sails), extended and waiting worshipfully before God in the solitary secret place and in fellowship with the saints. Whether alone or in fellowship with others, experiencing the heavenly places in Christ will satisfy that "da Vinci" longing within everyone. Nothing else will do. Our very capable wings of faith and knowledge of the Heavenly updrafts (the ways of the Holy Spirit) will take us there.

The keys to the Kingdom of God await you. Those keys will unlock the doors for your personal deliverance and healing, thereby unlocking the ministry of the same to others. It is time for you to fly.

Chapter III

Conquering the Resistance

Perfectly illustrated in the real-life story of the hawk, is this profound truth:

> *"The law of the Spirit of life in Christ Jesus has made me free from the law of sin and death" (Romans 8:2).*

The influence of the Spirit of God within the believer supersedes the law of sin and death just as the laws of lift and thrust supersede the law of gravity. By replacing the word "law" with "force" or "constraint," this liberating truth becomes clearer. Those two words acceptably define the use of the word "law" in this context.

Ignorance of this truth, and embracing the doctrines and traditions of men instead, will enslave you to a defeated low-level life. You should never allow anyone to cheat you of your God-given destiny or allow them to lessen your God-given means of fulfilling it (Colossians 2:8, 18). Failure to follow your Heavenly instinct will lead to a life in bondage to the fear of failure and the fear of man, resulting in unending and redundant toil—a cycle of mental and emotional ups and downs.

The believer in Christ is of a higher nature than those who are of the world. The roots of that nature largely consist of meekness and lowliness that cries out "Abba, Father God! You are everything my soul has ever longed for" (Romans 8:5; Galatians 4:6). That nature refuses to return evil for evil, bigotry for bigotry, and contempt for contempt, but instead, returns blessing for cursing. The world is not worthy of them and will never offer its applause. It is hostile to them and everything they represent. The believers in Christ belong to the heavenly places and will never feel at home in this world. If they fly too low, the "crows" will be there to remind them of where they belong. You are destined by the love the Father has set upon you to soar above the "crows," receiving whatever assurance, peace, joy, healing, deliverance, fatherly affirmation, purpose, or destiny is needed.

Although a hawk is born with a natural instinct to fly and hunt for prey, what if, contrary to its nature, a young hawk was consistently subject to restraints like a cage that would limit the use of its wings? Would its natural instinct to soar eventually become like a vague dream? **Imagine** if a hawk became confused and thought it belonged with the low flying birds instead or never had the example of other hawks concerning flight. Consequently, the hawk may never know a life without the harassment and wearing down of the "crows." The people of God must frequent the place of immunity in Christ or they will be worn down by their flesh, sin, the world, and the powers of darkness.

You can be lifted up to operate in the Spirit of Christ, His victorious life, or be worn down by those entities that know you are a threat to their existence.

What is your cage? Who or what are the low flying birds in your life? Have you lost sight of where you truly belong? Are you experiencing the heavenly places in Christ Jesus? Peter walked on water per Jesus' command but began to sink when he focused on and became fearful of the storm (Matthew 14:23-42). What are you focusing on that would cause your faith in Christ to sink? Did you know that when Jesus got into the boat, the sea became calm? This lesson burned this truth into the hearts of the disciples: the "storms" of life will test and prove our faith in Christ, uncovering any tendencies for us to focus on that which we cannot control, exposing our insecurities. After you are proven, the storm will end, ascertaining Christ's power over the very thing you found intimidating.

> *"The name of the Lord is a strong tower and the righteous run to it and are safe" (Proverbs 18:10).*

The word "safe" used in that verse can be translated "to be high; inaccessibly high." In Christ, you are inaccessibly high if you believe it. That was the reason it was translated "safe" in this instance. More accurately, you must not only acknowledge but also have a deep conviction of it and talk and behave accordingly. As the old song rightly says,

"Turn your eyes upon Jesus, look full in His wonderful face, and the things of earth will grow strangely dim in the light of His glory and grace."

Those who have true faith are in Him and He is in them. As you turn your focus on who He is (through meditation on Holy Scripture) with adoration, praise, and thanksgiving, you partake of His divine nature and find your wings. You can then soar in the reality of who you are in Him and who He is in you.

"But God, who is rich in mercy, because of His great love with which He loved us, (5) even when we were dead in trespasses, made us alive together with Christ (by grace you have been saved), (6) and raised us up together, and made us sit together in the heavenly places in Christ Jesus, (7) that in the ages to come He might show the exceeding riches of His grace in His kindness toward us in Christ Jesus" (Ephesians 2:4-7).

The force or constraint of the Spirit of life in Christ Jesus upon your life not only frees you from sin and death but also frees you unto God's service—unto being a formidable and precise instrument of His righteousness endowed with Heaven's hawk-like skill and perspective (Romans 6 & 8). So perfect is your position in the heavenly places in Christ that Jesus told His disciples:

> *"Behold, I give you the authority to trample on serpents and scorpions, and over all the power of the enemy, and nothing shall by any means hurt you" (Luke 10:19).*

Does "nothing" mean nothing?

Although Jesus told His disciples this before His death, resurrection, and ascension back to the Father, it was an introduction to New Covenant reality and experience, as was typical of His whole ministry on earth.

Jesus Christ, the Son of the living God, came from Heaven to earth to show us the way. Then He ascended back to Heaven by way of the cross and the grave. He has given us wings to ascend in this life, yet His life and ministry indicate that the way up is down. He said,

> *"Take My yoke upon you and learn from Me, for I am gentle and lowly in heart, and you will find rest for your souls" (Matthew 11:28-30).*

In order to take flight in Christ, you must first live with your knee bowed to His rest-giving lordship, the greatest characteristics of which are meekness and low-liness. His supreme lordship over all must be your deepest conviction, influencing every part of your life. Your wayward and self-willed soul must be convinced of its futile and wearing grind, of its false securities and comforts, and then surrender to the rest of Christ's lordship and learn of Him. Fleshly sin, self-righteousness, territorialism, false judgments, pride, and such things only give you a false sense of superiority and control. As do the crows, these things have the potential to cast down the "hawks" who have their longing eyes looking upward, searching for the updrafts in Christ.

We have been raised up together by grace, enabled by the Spirit (wind, breath) of God, not cast down by Him. Only those who exalt themselves shall be brought low by Him (Matthew 23:12; Luke 14:11, 18:14; James 4:6; 1 Peter 5:5). Due to the price Jesus paid and His resurrection from the grave, you get to use your wings of faith to explore and experience the vast blue sky of the heavenly places in Christ, as long as you stay humble before God and especially while the eyes of other people are admiring you—while you have their favorable attention. God never empowers self-effort, selfish-ambition, self-confidence, or self-exaltation, but inhabits and permeates faith in Christ's finished work and the consequent good fruit that comes from your life.

> *"For though the Lord is high, yet has He respect to the lowly [bringing them into fellowship with Him];*

> *but the proud and haughty He knows and recognizes*
> *[only] at a distance" (Psalms 138:6; TAB).*

You have been afforded the more-than-wonderful privilege of partaking of God's Divine nature (2 Peter 1:1-4). We have been raised up together from our lowly state and brought into fellowship with the Lord in is His high place. What wonders await the people of God! Is faith beginning to arise in your heart? Extend your wings toward Christ's great sacrificial love for you and catch the updraft of the Holy Spirit now.

I have seen Christians spend all their lives battling the devil but never truly overcoming. They have never come into the place of being inaccessibly high in Christ because the battle has become a distraction from their greatest priority. This is either because of ignorance, offense, self-righteousness, or because of their wrong beliefs concerning demonology and spiritual warfare. They are letting the "crows" distract them from true confidence in their hawk-like qualities and the continually available and accessible updrafts in Christ. The greatest defeat of the powers of darkness occurred at Jesus' death and resurrection. The book of Romans, chapter six, reveals that we died and rose with Him. If indeed Christ is in us and we are in Him, what is left to defeat? Complete surrender to Christ empowers you to defensively resist the powers of darkness and invasively enforce Christ's victory upon them, thereby destroying their works (James 4:7; 1 Peter 5:5-7; the whole book of Acts).

The powers of darkness have already heard you are coming to take down the "Jerichos" of this world. They are awaiting their doom. The demons cry out,

> *"What have we to do with You, Jesus, You Son of God? Have You come here to torment us before the time" (Matthew 8:29)?*

We are in Christ and He is in us, looking to do the same and greater works than He did during His ministry on earth.

Are you tired of battling the "crows" in your life? The wind is awaiting you! You can arise even if overcome with hopelessness. Arise now as God heals, delivers, affirms, and emboldens you against the downward and diabolical resistance. Arise in the likeness of the Son of God because you were predestined to be conformed to His image, to function in and release upon the earth the power of His redemptive love (Romans 8).

Chapter IV

The Crows' Union

Crows are territorial and easily threatened by the entrance of birds of prey. They keep a watchful eye over their domain and are unified by a community need to keep their territory safe. Their unity itself is an intimidating safeguard and weapon. Unified intimidation is their main weapon against those, such as hawks, who stray into their territory. Fear-based brotherhood works in nature for crows (and politics and the mafia) and serves as a catalyst for a "survival of the fittest" approach. Yet, this should never be found in any form among God's people.

For the believer in Christ, the goal of the powers of darkness is to preoccupy you with something besides the very thing for which you were created. Communing with Christ—partaking of His divine nature—is your greatest need and purpose in life. After obtaining and embracing this understanding, it can then become your greatest passion and pursuit. Like the hawk, you must understand that engaging the "crows" in life should never be your main priority or focus. You must turn your longing eyes toward the "sky" above.

Perspectives of and conclusions about your life experiences, other people, Biblical truth, the world, and God should only be formed from that vantage point.

Such things as observed in God's creation are intriguing, majestic, pure, and true. The hawk never became distracted, mesmerized, or bewildered by the crows' assault, but was dominated by its fierce natural instinct to soar above them. The hawk instead dealt with the crows on its own terms and level, instead of theirs. The hawk maintained the purity of what it is and did not allow the crows to muddy, diminish, or take advantage of it.

The crows found no vantage point against the hawk because the hawk gave them none.

Glory be to God! Pause right now and let this sink in deeply. Everything in me is crying out,

"Jesus, I am seated with you in the heavenly places because of your death, resurrection, and ascension. Your Holy Spirit is within and upon me to continually make that an experiential reality. I am like that hawk!"

As a believer in Christ, you must often take those kinds of pauses in life. These will facilitate what will be your defining moments—your sources of strength in the midst of the difficulties that can be used and choreographed by God to make you entirely dependent on Him and the "wings" He has given you.

Be careful though, there is another design of dark origins that seeks to ground you—to at least preoccupy your mind with something contrary to your Christ-like, heavenly nature.

Preoccupied, Ambitious, or Disillusioned?

The preoccupation could be a lot of "doing" instead of just "being" who you are in Christ. That "doing" begins to define you. If someone does not meet your expectations or volunteer to help you in your doing, you become offended and judge others as incompetent. Their help would never rise to the level of your perfectionism anyways (Luke 10:38-42). Martha learned she needed to be more like Mary, often sitting at Jesus' feet. She became so involved with service that her need to "fly" in communion with Christ became unfamiliar and vague like a forest path that has not been traversed for a long time. Never become so "busy" that you forget your only Source of eternal life—a quality of life that, when surrendered to, profoundly impacts every part of you.

Your most evident habits in life should reflect the need to commune with Christ.

Take some time now before the Lord and ask your-self as to how familiar you are with the ways of His Holy Spirit. For example, what are the nine gifts of the Spirit (1 Corinthians 12-14)? What are you not familiar with? Ask the Holy Spirit to help you experience the heavenly places in Christ Jesus.

You could also be caught up with the "sour grapes" that life has given you, trying to put out all the "little fires" started by "everyone's stupidity, sinfulness, and incompetency." You have become weary of doing it, realizing you are only making matters worse. Now you are ready to fully embrace this truth: God will not act on your behalf until you have sufficiently and worship-fully waited upon Him. Give up control and surrender to Christ's easy yoke.

Perhaps you are as Peter before Christ's crucifixion (Matthew 14). He was self-confident and then fell from that self-exalted place like a hawk without wings. He became greatly offended at himself because of failing Christ and had to be healed to go forward in life (John 21). Obviously, Peter was not as spiritually grounded as he thought.

> *"Therefore let him who thinks he stands take heed lest he fall" (1 Corinthians 10:12).*

Peter's devotion and loyalty to Christ was largely fu-eled by his own ambitions and enthusiasm. This is typi-cal for those of us (God's people) who are not acquainted enough with His truths and ways. Jesus had to address a competitive spirit among his disciples concerning who would be the greatest, and we must let those words address that competitiveness within us. Even as the hawk soars alone for one purpose, not being in competition with any other, so you must be single-minded—devoted only to explore the wondrous vast blue skies of who Christ is.

Imagine being one of Jesus' twelve, hearing His words, and seeing the many miracles. There was no lack of excitement—all of them were awed by everything Jesus said and did. It made them want to be just like Him in all of His greatness. Enthusiasm is not a bad thing. It is the fuel that empowers humanity to achieve and become great, at least in the world's estimation. The problem is that greatness itself is never something to be pursued in the Kingdom of God. It is only bestowed by Christ to those who aspire to be the greatest servants. They do not desire places of position or authority over people, but only boast in knowing their Father in Heaven. With Christ-like maturity, they seek to meekly serve God's purposes under the power and authority of the Holy Spirit instead. This precedent lays the groundwork upon which all church government must be built (Luke 22:25-27).

You can fruitlessly attempt to ascend the man-made hierarchal religious structures of the world in an attempt to achieve greater status before God or you can

easily explore the greatness of who Christ is with your
God-given abilities and status.

> *"Who may ascend into the hill of the LORD? Or
> who may stand in His holy place? (4) He who has
> clean hands and a pure heart, who has not lifted up his
> soul to an idol, nor sworn deceitfully. (5) He shall re-
> ceive blessing from the LORD, and righteousness from
> the God of his salvation" (Psalms 24-3-5).*

Our greatest enemy to soaring by grace through
faith into our place in Christ and experiencing all that
has been afforded us, is deceit. Deceit can easily take
captive the ignorant, the offended, the self-sufficient,
and the complacent.

Deceit often begins with disillusionment. Some syn-
onyms of "disillusionment" are: "disenchantment, disappointment, cynicism, letdown, discouragement, and
lacking in expectation." *The Oxford Dictionary* defines it
as, "A feeling of disappointment resulting from the dis-
covery that something is not as good as one believed
it to be." *The Merriam-Webster Dictionary* defines it as,
"To cause (someone) to stop believing that something
is good, valuable, true, etc." I would also add that it
includes a belief that God will do it for others but not
for you because of thinking you are a less-than. Let
me remind you of Cain before he killed Abel. Do you
have the Cain syndrome of feeling left out or of being
envious of others who seem to be God's favorites? Sur-

prise! God has no favorites. Those who honor God's ways will be honored by Him, and those who do not will not be honored by Him. It is as simple as that. What pleases God? Read Hebrews 11.

Disillusionment can lead to hopelessness just as it did with the very sick man who waited to be healed at the pool of Bethesda in John 5. He had no one to help put him in the pool after an angel would come down and disturb the waters. Only the first person in the pool afterward would be healed. Someone would always beat him to it. This was obviously an Old Covenant provision. Jesus Himself never condemned it as being anything less. He came up to the sick man and asked if he wanted to be healed. Why would Jesus ask him a question to which the answer was obvious? Because sickness can become for any of us, a focal point from which we attract human pity. Receiving human pity can become somewhat like an addictive drug to us because it ministers a little psychological relief from the suffering. Jesus, however, was and is the completion of the Old Covenant, its provision, and observances. He is the fullness of the Godhead embodied. While introducing the sick man to the New Covenant, Jesus presented Himself as the end to his need to depend on those things that were limited in their ability to make him well.

Now, oh hopeless one, you can look to Christ who speaks and releases us from the chains of

hopelessness! Arise, from your bed of despair and walk. Bless the Lord with all that is within you and you will begin to not only walk but to fly.

The devil's weapon of disillusionment often begins with your being tempted into believing that you are better off going at it alone because people, including Church leaders, are not dependable. Perhaps you became disillusioned because of expecting too much from people without having a strong personal relationship with your Father in Heaven. That is a recipe for pain.

Possibly, your believing in something good that was supposed to happen was not the problem. You also need to understand that just believing it does not turn it into a good experience. The woman with the issue of blood (never-ending menstrual cycle) had to press through the crowd to get to Jesus and be healed (Matthew 9:20-22). Blind Bartimaeus had to cry out to receive his healing and continued to do so even louder while people were telling him to be quiet (Mark 10:46-52). Against his pride and prejudice, Naaman, the Syrian commander, had to dip in the Jordan River seven times to be healed from leprosy (2 Kings 5:1-14).

The number seven in Scripture is often used to signify the completion of a thing. God desires and requires perfect (completed) faith in Him and obedience to His instructions. At times, he may require something that grates against our likes, dislikes, and "better judgment." However, it will never be difficult while doing it. God will not require anything from us without empowering us to do it. You also must seek the Lord for His instructions and follow them to prove your obedient faith in Him and receive what you need.

In the Old Testament (Exodus 29), priests who were to serve in the temple had to be consecrated to the Lord for seven days. They began the process of following the Lord's instructions concerning their consecration, but He always completed it with His manifest glory as promised. What we begin in obedience to the Lord's specific instructions, He will finish much to our benefit.

I remember while ministering in a church in Texas back around the turn of the century, a woman received a healing from non-functioning bowels. Her bowels started working after the meeting. Later, the Lord told her that she needed to change her eating habits if she wanted to stay healed. Well, she did so and remained healed (to my knowledge). Likewise, we must always follow the Lord's instructions before and after.

What have you been deceived into believing about God, other people, the world, and yourself? That which originates from sin-infected humanity, whether good, bad, political, or religious is designed to one end, to undo your faith in Christ. The diabolical goal is either to keep you from having a full assurance of faith in God or to redirect it to something of human/demonic origin. For the true believer in Christ, the goal of the crow-type deceit would be to take advantage of a weakness, causing your faith in those things that are already yours in Christ to fade (1 Corinthians 2:12). Those things are not just for a privileged few who are super-Christians. The ability to fly and soar on the updrafts of Christ's grace sum up those things and are continually available and immediately accessible to those who follow God's protocol (Hebrews 10). That protocol is summed up in this: Christ's shed blood affords us a full assurance of faith and spiritual heart purity by which we can draw near to God. If we lack the confidence and determination, both can be restored through thanksgiving that focuses solely on Christ's finished work on the cross and His resurrection.

Those who are hawks in Christ must never allow the powers of darkness to lure them into attributing more power to the downward pull of the things of this world than to the upward pull of the law of the Spirit of life in Christ Jesus.

Chapter V

Unshakable Confidence

If a hawk, contrary to its nature, allowed outward things to mold it into what it can be and do, it would never get off the ground. It would be trained in harmony with and in conformity to the downward pull of the surroundings that it should be conquering.

You should never let the outward things of this world dictate who you are and what you are going to do. That should only be determined by the upward call and claim on your life by the Lord. The hawk was born as a predator to conquer the vast blue skies. You were reborn by God Himself to conquer. He is the Creator and sustainer of the heavens and the earth and never faints or becomes weary. That same inexhaustible and conquering life of Christ is in all of those who believe. His Spirit will envelop and flow out of anyone who worshipfully waits before Him for their wings (Isaiah 40).

"And do not be conformed to this world, but be transformed by the renewing of your mind, that you may prove what is that good and acceptable and perfect will of God" (Romans 12:2).

Can you identify those things that actually prop up your self-worth, self-image, and identity? The source for such things will determine the stability of them and, ultimately, your overall stability and integrity.

From where does your spiritual confidence or strength come? What is it and how does it practically effect your behavior?

For two consecutive mornings, I was awakened by the Lord while He was writing words on my forehead with His finger. Among other things, the word "strength" was engraved there.

"He gives power to the weak, and to those who have no might He increases strength" (Isaiah 40:29).

According to Isaiah 40:28-30, three prerequisites are necessary for receiving God's strength:

- You have to be weak and/or have deep convictions that you are weak apart from Christ (v. 29).

- You cannot be self-dependent, as in: dependencies on youthful strength, your own intelligence, natural birthright, other claims-to-fame that may exist, or whatever fleeting securities prop up your self-image, worth, esteem, and identity (v. 30).

• As a lifestyle, you must worshipfully wait on the everlasting God, the **LORD**, the Creator of the ends of the earth, who neither faints nor is weary (vs. 28, 31).

Worshipfully waiting on the Lord may initially involve dealing with those things that have misdirected or distracted your faith. Allow the Holy Spirit to shine His light on them, or you will hardly get off the ground.

The outcome of every battle you will face in this life is determined by this: what you believe concerning God's approval of you. That approval is based solely on your obedient faith in Christ's finished work. From that comes the spiritual resilience and fierceness to overcome in every battle.

Scripture has declared:

> *"Blessed is the man to whom the Lord will not impute sin [disobedience to God's moral law]" (Romans 4:8).*

This truth secures our identity, self-worth, and purpose in life down to the deepest levels of our humanity. Those who are secure in these things will not easily be undone by criticism, praise or flattery, difficulties, or temptations of any kind.

> *"Whoever comes to Me, and hears My sayings and does them, I will show you whom he is like: (48) He is like a man building a house, who dug deep and laid the foundation on the rock. And when the flood arose, the stream beat vehemently against that house, and could not shake it, for it was founded on the rock"* *(Luke 6:47-49).*

As Jesus warned, we must dig to the rock—to the place of spiritual, mental, and emotional solidity, stability, and integrity. The rock in Christ is the place where we know without a doubt we have God's life-giving approval. It is the place where you not only come to understand God's word but also hear Him speak directly to you concerning His love and plan for you. You will then understand what the Apostle John was indicating when he said,

> *"But the anointing which you have received from Him abides in you, and you do not need that anyone teach you; but as the same anointing teaches you concerning all things, and is true, and is not a lie, and just as it has taught you, you will abide in Him"* *(1 John 2:27).*

This truth reiterated one of three New Covenant promises in Hebrews 8:11 which states, "None of them shall teach his neighbor, and

none his brother, saying, 'Know the LORD,' for all shall know Me, from the least of them to the greatest of them."

In that place, the Father will affirm you by His voice. Your hawk-like abilities will become quite evident as He covers you with His feathers (Psalms 91). While your impassioned heart listens inwardly for the Father's voice, your longing eyes will be looking skyward.

You must dig or search out the solidity of who Christ is; otherwise, your foundation is sand and will be easily undone by hardship. The digging entails uncovering what is hidden from those who never diligently search. How important was finding the rock to the builder? It was the priority before anything else. Even so, we must continually find the solidity of who Christ is in the secret place. This is how we find our wings and arise from this world's downward pull and soar to safety.

The "digging" described here is not a difficult thing because that is exactly what you have been doing while reading this book.

Since God loves us just as He loves Jesus, how do we continually experience that reality? First, by incorporating and rehearsing it within our way of thinking and belief system—digging to the rock. Your having believed that God raised Jesus from the dead invoked God's life-giving approval upon and within you. Though you were dead because of sin, deserving eternal punishment, God made you alive in Christ. He made you alive unto Himself; having made you aware of Him and the good He intends toward you. This awareness includes His forgiveness of your sins and His fatherly covenant-love for you. This truth will be continually rehearsed and commemorated by God's people throughout the ages to come (The book of Revelation). How much more should we rehearse it in this present evil age? Jesus said that we are to commemorate His death and resurrection as often as we will by way of the symbolic cup and bread of the Lord's Supper (Luke 22:14-20; 1 Corinthians 23-26). Take note that the bread and wine of the Lord's Supper are not just symbols. They are points of contact in this physical realm by which your faith is able to link the seen with the unseen, thereby reaping the eternal benefits of Christ's finished work. Jesus said, as was confirmed by the Apostle Paul, *"Eat...drink for this is My body of the new covenant."* As you believe, so you will receive.

> *"For let not that man [the one who doubts] suppose that he will receive anything from the Lord; (8) he is a double-minded man, unstable in all his ways"* (James 1:7-8).

> *"If you can believe, all things are possible to him who believes"* (Mark 9:23).

"With men this is impossible, but with God all things are possible" (Matthew 19:26).

There are some things that are possible with men, as Jesus implied, but all things are possible with God. The world is full of modern marvels of human invention and genius that can become obstacles to receiving from God. The more you marvel at the glory of withering flesh (Isaiah 40:6-8), the more indistinct the wonders of the unseen and eternal realm of God become. The more faith you place in this world system, the more foreign and even foolish the things of God become to you (Romans 8:5-8; 1 Corinthians 1). From that unseen and eternal realm, God answers your impossibilities in His Son. Jesus is the same as He was on earth (Hebrews 13:8). His compassion and mercies do not fail. He does not withhold New Covenant blessings but does reserve the right to chastise His own people (Hebrews 12). His chastisement aims at keeping you from being cheated of those blessings. Ask your Father in Heaven to reveal anything of rebellion, stubbornness, offense, unforgiveness, or self-rule in your life. These will keep you from receiving His answers to your impossibilities. These will keep you at ground level.

With God, all things are possible, so you must be with Him and not working against Him. His promises are for those who are far away and to those who are near. He will close the distance. Just take that first step and believe He will give you wings.

"Draw near to Him and He will draw near to you"
(James 4:8).

Oh, how blessed are those to whom God accredits no sin! How can this be? That is how effective and powerful the blood of Christ is. It has so much appeal, power, and influence before God's throne that He considers those who place faith therein as if they had never sinned. This is why the book of Hebrews (chapter 10) warns us, God's people, about not neglecting, despising, or abusing that precious blood of the Lamb. Those who do so could receive worse punishment than those who despised Moses' law under the Old Covenant.

From the precious blood of the Lamb comes your spiritual purity, strength, courage, and boldness. From that blood comes your right of passage to everything you need for reigning as Jesus did in this life and in the one to come. From that blood and the purity of mind and conscience it creates within arises your right of passage to the vast blue skies of all that has been given to us in Christ (Matthew 5:8; 1 Corinthians 2:12). Are you rejoicing with me? Either fall on your face right now or stand up, shout, and dance (or all of the above). Jesus is alive for evermore within you and me and is Lord of all! His indwelling, conquering life causes me to soar!

The hawk was born with the purity of what it was designed to be and do. Likewise, our rebirth in Christ and our having received the Holy Spirit

as they did on Pentecost (Acts 2) has equipped us to conquer the downward pull of this world and soar as more than conquerors above it.

Strong, unshakable confidence is maintained by you actively and continually showering Christ's redeeming love on others. Doing this incorporates, among other things, acts of fierce compassion and Holy Spirit-inspired declarations of the uncompromised truth.

> *"Blessed are the pure in heart for they shall see God"*
> *(Matthew 5:8).*

Like a hawk in flight, there is a purity of heart that searches with keen spiritual vision from its great vantage point in Christ. It seeks out places in this world where it can release the forgiveness of sin and redemptive love upon the great masses of people, thereby causing evil to turn backward upon itself. Those releases begin with declarations of forgiveness and mercy upon those who are oblivious to the reality of who Christ is. As Jesus did just before He died, you must release forgiveness and mercy upon those who are hostile toward God—those who would seek to kill the righteous if certain restraints were lifted.

This great vantage point you have in Christ is NOT a place for attitudes of condescension or self-righteousness. We forfeit that vantage point when we sit on our self-made pedestal like a vulture waiting for the "carcass" to die so we can tear at its flesh. The hawks in

Christ should never lower themselves to act like vultures or else they will only get the vultures reward—the rotting flesh (carnality) of their victims (corruption; Galatians 6:8). To be carnally minded is death and chaos but to be spiritually minded is life and peace (Romans 8:6).

Your flight in Christ is unto this end: your enjoyment and to disperse the seeds of Christ's serpent-killing love throughout the earth.

Do you want to see the powers of darkness and their conquests thwarted and even paralyzed? Do you want to see the serpent of cultural offense and hate defanged? You must believe that the power of Christ's redemptive love far exceeds the power of the hostility that exists toward God in the earth. Declare forgiveness even toward those you feel no animosity toward instead of speaking condescending words. Refuse to associate or be affiliated with those who are behaving like vultures.

The greatest victories the body of Christ will see in the earth will only happen when we perfect this.

Chapter VI

The Power of Righteousness

Even the Old Covenant in its imperfections (Hebrews 7) was able to secure for the Israelites a most blessed state before God and their enemies. Listen to the Prophet Balaam, who was not an Israelite, as he prophesied over Israel (Numbers 23):

> *"How shall I curse whom God has not cursed? And how shall I denounce whom the LORD has not denounced? (9) For from the top of the rocks I see him, and from the hills I behold him; There! A people dwelling alone, not reckoning itself among the nations. (10) Who can count the dust of Jacob, or number one-fourth of Israel? Let me die the death of the righteous, and let my end be like his!"*

> *"Behold, I have received a command to bless; He has blessed, and I cannot reverse it. (21) He has not observed iniquity in Jacob, nor has He seen wickedness in Israel. The LORD his God is with him, and the shout of a King is among them. (22) God brings them*

out of Egypt; He has strength like a wild ox. (23)
For there is no sorcery against Jacob, nor any divi-
nation against Israel. It now must be said of Jacob
and of Israel, 'Oh, what God has done!' (24) Look,
a people rises like a lioness, and lifts itself up like a
lion; it shall not lie down until it devours the prey, and
drinks the blood of the slain."

Similar to the hawk soaring the skies in its God-giv-
en purity and majesty, Israel soared with God in the
experiential reality of the full blessings of the blood
covenant. God's covenant blessing had made them the
dread and envy of the nations. As Balaam looked out
over the encampment of Israel in the valley below, he
caught a glimpse of a people upon whom God's favor
completely rested. He beheld such splendor that left
him in awe of the God of Israel. He was not an Israelite
by birth but wanted to be one of them. The "da Vinci"
longing arose within his heart—that same longing you
and I have of wanting to be like the hawk illustrated in
this book. The Spirit of God came upon him and he
spoke forth this revelation as it filled his heart. Balaam
understood that no nation on earth could withstand Israel and no curse could vex them. They had the shout
(authority) of the King of Kings among them. It became obvious to Balaam that Israel was the lion predator among the nations, and all others were the prey.

Oh, but this story has a dark side. While such insight could have served as an invitation from God for

Balaam to become one of His people, he instead used it against them and chose to become a crow (or vulture) rather than a hawk. He understood that the above was only true as long as God did not observe or see iniquity and wickedness in their camp. So, Balaam, in his greed and wickedness, used this knowledge against Israel and taught Balak, king of Moab, to seduce them to step outside of God's favor and blessing. He taught this desperate, wicked king how to turn God against Israel in judgment. The children of Israel, in their naivety, were seduced into compromising their high position in the Lord through unholy conduct. Their shout no longer had clout with God. The crows' evil crusade was accomplished. It took the zeal and Godly fear (angry compassion; fierceness) of Phinehas to restore God's authority, favor, and blessing back to Israel. God used him to reinstate the importance of holiness among His people. In fact, the entirety of the Old Covenant was dedicated to establishing this one thing in the earth: the importance of God's holiness.

There are no people in the earth who can compare to those who are righteous before God—people to whom God does not accredit sin. Absolutely nothing can harm them. No army can defeat them. No one (including the devil) can successfully (or legally) bring a charge (accusation) against them (Romans 8). If God is for them, then who can be against them? If He has blessed them, then who can curse them? Under His protection, who can even come near them with evil intent? Anything that would bring sickness, disease, harm, or calamity into their lives is held back because of the righteousness that is of faith. They soar like the hawk in those places in Christ where the crows cannot go. However, if they compromise holiness, take up offense, become complacent, begin to strive in their flesh, lean on their own understanding, and do not entirely depend on the righteousness that is of faith, then the devil will gain a foothold or vantage point of oppression in their lives. Listen to Solomon:

> *"Trust in the LORD with all your heart, and lean not on your own understanding; (6) in all your ways acknowledge Him, and He shall direct your paths. (7) Do not be wise in your own eyes; fear the LORD and depart from evil. (8) It will be health to your flesh, and strength to your bones" (Proverbs 3:5-8).*

Quiet times in the secret place will often be necessary for the hawks in Christ to regain their spiritual bearings and to refocus their trust only in the Lord.

Why? Because there are "Balaams" out there who are planning your demise.

Periods of giving your undivided attention unto acknowledging Christ in all of your ways will be necessary to remain healthy. Your flight equipment must be maintained. Your protective feathers must be oiled (anointed).

When we look away from the Author and Finisher of our faith, our great vantage point over the powers of darkness will slip away from us. We will lose sight of the fact that we belong to the "vast blue sky" of all that Christ is.

We **are** seated with Christ in the heavenly places *now*. This is not a future event. This great vantage point is a place of immunity that can only be realized and experienced by our surrendering to grace and walking by faith. Only by grace through faith will we enjoy the benefits thereof. God will sustain and strengthen us as a soaring hawk and lion predator through His righteousness, and reassure, affirm, console, and instruct us by His fathering grace.

Listen to the psalmist:

> *"Truly my soul silently waits for God; from Him comes my salvation. (2) He only is my rock and my salvation; He is my defense; I shall not be greatly moved [to totter, shake, or slip]. (3) How long will you attack a man? You shall be slain, all of you, like a leaning wall and a tottering fence. (4) They only consult to cast him down from his high position; they delight in lies; they bless with their mouth, but they curse inwardly. Selah" (Psalms 62:1-4).*

This Scripture passage closely parallels and applies to the human experiential level the event I witnessed between the hawk and crows. Notice the psalmist said in verse two that he would not be greatly moved. For some reason, he did not have complete confidence in the Lord, or else he would have stated that he would not be moved, period. Something took place that left his faith in God in a weakened state. Then he turned and addressed his enemies (vs. 3-4), having received a revelation from God. He realized there was an attempt by his adversaries to "cast him down from his high position" (v. 4). After he regained his focus on the Lord, the psalmist was then able to see his foes for what they really were and not what they appeared to be. The psalmist turned to his enemies, addressed them accordingly, and then worshiped God.

> *"My soul, wait thou only upon God; for my expectation is from him. (6) He only is my rock and my salvation: he is my defense;* **I shall not be moved**" *(Psalms 62:5-6).*

His confidence was restored. Remember what happens to those who worshipfully wait on the Lord according to Isaiah 40:31?

On a National Geographic television presentation entitled The Great Barrier Reef, a bigger fish stealthily approaches a smaller one, inhales, and the smaller fish disappears into the predator's jaws. But wait, within a matter of seconds, the big fish spits its prey. Why? Because the small fish was equipped with the ability to inflate at least twice its size. This skill serves as its main defense, thus making it impossible for some larger fish to swallow. The whole point here is that the smaller fish was able to appear much larger than it really was. Likewise, the powers of darkness can appear to be more powerful, intimidating, threatening, and oppressive than they really are. How do you think that the devil went from being a serpent in the book of Genesis to a dragon in the book of the Revelation? The devil is able to inflate himself through the fleshly pride of men who are trying to be like God apart from God. Scripture testifies that such wickedness would increase in the last days (Matthew 24:12). Even so, the serpent's appearance has bloated to deceive and control the masses of people.

How intimidating can two crows be to a hawk in flight? Not at all, if the hawk remembers who it is and what it has been equipped with.

The devil's focal point of attack is to undermine your faith so that you will slip, totter, or be shaken from your high position in Christ, thus making him in appearance to be as a dragon that flies overhead instead of a serpent that is under your feet. All of his attacks against God's people are ultimately designed unto this end. This is why we are to always have a resistant, sober, and watchful attitude towards the devil and his direct assaults against us (1 Peter 5:8-9; James 4:7-8). If we stay submitted to God, He will enable us to know deeply that the devil is an already judged and defeated foe. We can then triumph over him and his works in every sphere of life from a position of resting or almost effortlessly soaring in Christ's finished work and victory (the heavenly places in Christ). In submitting to God, He will give us a strategy on how to deal with the devil. Satan will flee as a result, taking his destructive works with him without exception. If we meet God's conditions and follow His instructions, He will fulfill His promises.

> *"For, if by the one man's offense death reigned through the one, how much more will those who receive abundance of grace and of the gift of righteousness reign in life through the One, Jesus Christ" (Romans 5:17; adapted for clarity).*

Over what are you to reign in this life? Well, what did Jesus reign over? His flesh and the works of the devil, of course. This reigning referred to is not accomplished by great effort and focus, but by (super) naturally soaring with Christ in the heavenly places—in the place of complete surrender and trust in His great sustaining love. Like the hawk, you simply do what you were originally created to do.

You must obtain an abundance of grace to maintain personal holiness and the purity of who God has made you. Having a firm grasp on the gift of righteousness will secure continual victory and cause you to arise even from demoralizing failure. Since God only gives grace to the humble, then only those who walk humbly with God are qualified to reign in this life over everything contrary to His perfect will—everything Jesus came to destroy. His will toward us was proven through Christ's ministry on earth and made surer through His death and resurrection.

> *"For this purpose the Son of God was manifested, that He might destroy the works of the devil" (1 John 3:8).*

Abundant grace enables or empowers us to reign, and the gift of righteousness gives us the right to reign.

We must, therefore, make sure that we are not treating others contrary to the testimony of Christ's precious blood in Heaven. Through His blood alone are we made righteous before God. It always speaks in our behalf and never against us. Consequently, our lives must bear the aroma of His sacrifice, displaying His redeeming love. Anything less is complacency or self-righteousness, and we will, as the result, forfeit our right to reign in life through Christ.

Our high position in Christ has nothing to do with showing disrespect toward the powers of darkness, calling them degrading names, or having a haughty attitude. Even Michael the Archangel, who is far more powerful than us, does not bring reviling accusations against the devil (Jude 1:9). If we will remain in the place of brokenness (softness of heart), the Christ-like fierceness toward the spiritual powers of darkness and love for the Church and the world will become our immunity against anything the devil can throw at us. When God's love flows out of you, nothing can swim upstream and you will walk in an authority to which all hell will bow the knee. That love cannot flow if your peace with God is undone within you (Romans 5:1-2). If you are caught up with how messed up or how good you or someone else is, then you have lost sight of that blessed state accredited to those who believe that Jesus is alive from the grave.

You must remain in the shadow of the cross (God's love revealed) if you are going to love in the same way. Those who lay down their lives out of love for others, even as Jesus did for His enemies, will experience the full blessing of their high place in Christ. Otherwise, your confidence in the Lord will totter. Your hawk-like "wings" of faith will lose the ability to soar. Jesus' greatest defeat over the powers of darkness was not by direct confrontation, but by His death. That death was love revealed in its greatest splendor. Perfect love defeated supreme wickedness. Likewise, your co-death with Christ (the laying down of your life) will be the catalyst used by God to destroy the works of darkness.

> *"Be excellent in what is good, innocent of evil, and the God of peace will soon crush Satan underneath your feet" (Romans 16:19-20; paraphrased).*

This is why you must have an abundance of grace and the gift of righteousness in order to reign in this life. Notice, and this is important, you do not achieve an abundance of grace and the gift of righteousness. You receive it instead! Yes, you have to rightly position yourself to receive it, but must first be convinced of its availability and accessibility. It takes an abundance of grace in order for you to walk in love toward all, laying down your life, and thereby maintain your confidence, and your high position in Christ. If your heart condemns you, because you did not remain in Christ's love, your confidence will falter (see 1 John 3:16-24). You must, therefore, default to the finished work of the cross to retain peace with God, **with yourself, and your fellowman.**

Have you become weary in maintaining your high position in Christ? Do you feel comparable to a "leaning wall and tottering fence?" Has the devil been trying to wear you out and cast you down? Be encouraged this day for greater is He that is in you than he who is in the world. Look unto the Author and Finisher of your faith, and then, as did the psalmist, you will see that all your enemies are like leaning walls and tottering fences. You will watch as they give up in their pursuit of you as with the hawk and the annoying crows. Spending a "season" in prayer and fasting may be necessary to see and experience the victory, but it will come. Never forget to look for opportunities to help others who are downcast, and you will reap, in due season, if you faint not and will know without doubt that the prince of this world is judged (John 16:7-11). You will soar above the deluge that comes from the mouth of the dragon—his mesmerizing accusations against the people of God (Revelation 12). Let your giving to others be defined by God's love and not by the limitations of flawed human love and expectation. Put on the Lord Jesus Christ, for He alone is your righteousness, and make no provision for the flesh to fulfill its lusts (Romans 13:14).

Begin now to praise Him for His gift of righteousness, and you will come into an abundance of grace.

Give thanks for the Lamb who has taken away your sins. By so doing, your enemies will totter and fall! You will be able to say with full assurance and finality as the psalmist,

"I shall not be moved! Like the hawk, I am soaring in Christ's surpassing victory! His breath sustains me."

The breathtaking love of Christ that surrendered to the greatest of evil as a lamb to be slaughtered for the sins of the world is now roaring as the Lion of the Tribe of Judah. Let Him roar through you.

Epilogue

Have you enjoyed the journey?

What an incredible way to describe the rewards and features we have in Christ as seen in the real-life example of the hawk that always followed its natural instinct. The main difference with us is that we have a God-given "super" natural instinct. The human race lost its way in the beginning (Genesis). Now, we have Christ Jesus who was sent by the Father as the Way, Truth, and Life (John 14). Those who arise in Him, having also been filled with the Holy Spirit, are destined to turn the world upside down, as it was said of the early Christians (Acts 17).

No matter what your sphere of influence is or what your past and present state is, whether you are hopeful or hopeless, Christ's voice has gone out to you. He has called out to the whole earth saying,

> *"If anyone thirsts, let him come to Me and drink. (38) He who believes in Me, as the Scripture has said, out of his heart will flow rivers of living water" (John 7:37-38; Romans 10).*

Complete satisfaction that leaves nothing undone within you has already been offered from Heaven. No one will be able to stand before God on Judgment Day and blame Him nor boast in his or her own, nor any-one's reputation.

Jesus said that your Heavenly Father is in the secret place and that every one of us is called to meet with Him there (Matthew 6:15-21). This is your highest call-ing of all. What rewards are awaiting those who do? From where have you been seeking rewards? What is your value system based on? Is it in what people think of you, how much money you are making, or whether you are in a relationship with a certain someone? As for me, I am pursuing the Heavenly rewards that the Father will make evident to everyone around us so that they too will unequivocally value the unseen eternal things of God. Come with me.

Failures, shortcomings, and a lack of wisdom are unsurpassable walls only to the doubters. If you be-lieve, these are opportunities for God to reveal His glo-ry, displacing your weakness with His strength, your sorrow and sadness with His joy, and your human lim-itations with His limitlessness. Therefore, we, as Paul, should glory in our weaknesses, adversities, and failures (2 Corinthians 12). This means you should see them as opportunities for your Father to reveal His splendor.

Understand that a young hawk has to start using its wings in order to experience the won-ders of the heavens above. Its start is never per-fect, but its skills are improved by using them.

Those similar skills in you will progress and become like breathing and an instinct by practice. Those skills are customized for you and are far more inviting than a very comfortable and warm overcoat in the cold of winter.

Wheat begins as a blade or seedling. After time, the grain head appears, and finally, the full grain is grown (Mark 4:28). In this life, we begin and end our journey in the Kingdom of God as discoverers—seeking out what we have inherited as joint heirs with Christ.

> *"Ask, and it will be given to you; seek, and you will find; knock, and it will be opened to you" (Luke 11:9).*

There is much to be discovered no matter our level of spiritual maturity. Whether you have just begun the journey or have already made many discoveries searching and soaring in the heavenly places in Christ, your Father in Heaven is very determined to take you from faith to faith, strength to strength, and glory to glory. He desires that you do not stay on one level of development for too long because of the pending dangers of doing so (Romans 1:17; Psalms 84:1-7; 2 Corinthians; Hebrews 5-6; 1 Peter 5:5-9).

Your Father in Heaven will not scold you for what you lack. Although, He will hold you accountable for what you have been given in Christ to overcome the downward pull of this world. He gives you much grace, including the necessary correction that you need to develop and mature unto Christ's image.

The Old Testament Prophet Elijah was a man who prayed fervently for no rain and later for rain, and God granted both (1 Kings 18; James 5:17-18). The effective and fervent prayers of the righteous profit much. There were no clouds in the sky when Elijah first heard the sound of abundance of rain. That is odd. How can someone hear rain before it actually appears? This indicates that the Holy Spirit was showing him in the unseen realm of God what He had already planned to do. In accordance with what the Father reveals to you in secret, He will also openly reward you. Through Holy Spirit-inspired insight and effective, fervent praying, you too can witness even nature itself bow its knee to Christ. Seven times (the number in the Bible that represents completion) Elijah prayed until he could actually see a cloud form.

Prayer asks for rain but faith carries an umbrella. The prayer of faith with thanksgiving keeps pursuing until its obedience is (seven times) complete—until the umbrella it carries is needed.

Many have tried to mount up against life's hardships and challenges in their own strength only to fail or give up. The reason for which is that the understanding of God's ways was not first secured before Heaven's answer arrived. They that worshipfully wait upon the Lord will renew their strength and will mount up with wings that come from Him. They will hear the sound of an abundance of whatever is applicable, in tune with God's heart, before it actually appears and will be rewarded openly. Do you now hear the sound?

We serve a Heavenly Father who can do extraordinarily beyond anything we can imagine according to the power that works in us (Ephesians 3:20). Do you believe? Mount up with your wings and discover the possibilities. All things are possible to them that believe.

When His disciples asked Him to increase their faith (Luke 17), Jesus replied:

> *"If you have faith as a mustard seed, you can say to this mulberry tree, 'Be pulled up by the roots and be planted in the sea,' and it would obey you. (7) And which of you, having a servant plowing or tending sheep, will say to him when he has come in from the field, 'Come at once and sit down to eat'? (8) But will he not rather say to him, 'Prepare something for my supper, and gird yourself and serve me till I have eaten and drunk, and afterward you will eat and drink'? (9) Does he thank that servant because he did the things that were commanded him? I think not. (10) So likewise you, when you have done all those things which you are commanded, say, 'We are*

*unprofitable servants.   We have done what was our
duty to do.'"*

In order for their faith to be increased, Jesus first
told them that they needed faith like a mustard seed.
This is not the same mustard seed we are familiar with
in America. In Eastern Asia, this seed produces a plant
that can reach heights of over ten feet. Who would
think that such a small seed could produce a plant that
reaches the height of a tree? It would be very easy
to underestimate or disregard the seed if you had no
knowledge of what produced it and what was inside of
it. In order for faith to be increased, the seeds of God's
incorruptible words of faith, as revealed in New Covenant promises and the person and ministry of Christ,
must never be underestimated, disregarded, or under
valued by you. Just think about it: what is the inherent
potential of one seed? How many times can it repro-
duce itself one generation after the next? The possibilities are almost limitless. When we begin to value
Christ's words in like manner, nothing will be impossible to us.

But wait, Jesus had more to say about increasing
your faith. You must be like that servant whose whole
life was spent for one purpose: to make sure your Master
is taken care of first, not even expecting a "thank-you"
while doing so. The servant does this for one reason: he
or she knows the Master is worthy. That servant knows
that by living with such single-mindedness, he or she

will not need to be concerned about his or her own welfare. The servant has given up his or her temporal concerns in exchange for their Master's eternal purposes. That servant does not spend his or her days worrying about the things of this life but has the deep assurance of the Master's provision as an obedient servant should. He or she does not live to serve the self-life, other people, or the things of this world.

Those who have such a servant's attitude will soar in the high altitudes in Christ. They can arise with their hawk-like abilities and abide under the shadow of the Almighty (Psalms 91).

> *"Oh, taste and see that the LORD is good; blessed is the man who trusts in Him" (Psalms 34:8)!*

Whatever eye-catching thing you focus on will stir within you both passion and desire for it. Do you sense holy desire stirring within you for the things of God? The more you taste, the more you want. The more you walk this earth, the more your longing eyes will turn skyward. Is new passion arising within your heart? The Lord desires that your righteousness be as the shining of the dawn and your salvation as a torch that burns (Isaiah 62:1-5). Imagine a bridegroom rejoicing over his bride who is passionately in love with him. The Lord wants to rejoice over you in like manner! (v.5). This God-given righteousness and salvation you possess must be heated by the flames of righteous desire for the

Bridegroom. Only then will it profoundly impact the world. Then you will not become weary, but will mount up with your wings and soar in the realities for which you were created.

Arise to your place, people of God, with love set aflame by righteous desire and fierce compassion.

"...As He [Christ] is, so are we in this world" (1 *John 4:17).*

About the Author

Gary, along with his wife Teresa, is a 1986 graduate of Christ for the Nations Bible College in Dallas, Texas. He is an author and has preached the word of God since 1982. He is also working on publishing other books. He and his wife founded Great Grace Revival Ministries in 1995 and have both served as pastors, elders, and prophetic voices in the local church and as part of ministry teams. With a passion to see God's people rooted and grounded in Holy Bible truth, he and his wife desire to work with others in bringing another "Great Awakening" in the USA and other nations. This involves implementing God's initiatives through prayer and powerful and precise declarations of His word with signs, wonders, and miracles of the Holy Spirit.

Contact Information

grace4u@gmx.com

http://www.greatgrace4u.com

www.ingramcontent.com/pod-product-compliance
Lightning Source LLC
Chambersburg PA
CBHW071827020426
42331CB00007B/1632